KU-350-593

This UK and Commonwealth Edition by
Schofield & Sims Limited Publishers ©1995
Series by Françoise Detay-Lanzmann and Nicole Hibert
Illustrations by Daniel Moignot
First published by Editions Mango, Paris ©1995

0 7217 5015 X

FIRST IMPRESSIONS

How they Grow

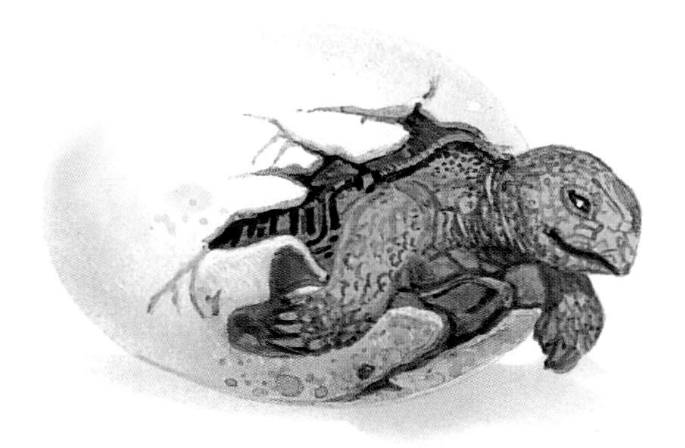

Schofield & Sims Limited Huddersfield.

The Cat

A kitten is born with its eyes closed. They begin to open after about a week. At first, a kitten's eyes are blue, but they change colour as the kitten grows older.

After 3 weeks, the kittens start to stand up and take their first steps. Soon afterwards, teething begins.

The cat carries her kittens for about 9 weeks before giving birth. Each kitten is born in a small pouch of fluid. The mother cat breaks this open so the kitten does not suffocate. She then bites through the *umbilical cord* with her teeth and licks the kitten clean.

By the time a kitten is 8 weeks old, it will be *weaned*. It starts to lose its milk teeth at 12 weeks.

When it plays, the kitten learns all the movements of hunting. It lies in wait to pounce on its toy and 'kill' it, just as it will do later on with mice. At one year old, a kitten has become an adult.

The Duck

As soon as they are born, the chicks rub themselves against their mother's oily feathers. This makes their fine, soft down become *impermeable* to water.

Some hours after they are born, the ducklings leave the nest and follow their mother on to the pond in search of insects and *larvae*.

In the spring, the female lays between 7 and 16 eggs in her nest, which is usually built on dry ground. When they are ready to hatch, the chicks break through their shells.

hen danger threatens her young, the other duck stretches out her neck and acks very loudly. The chicks mediately dive under the water.

When they are 8 weeks old, the ducklings start to fly. By autumn, they will be adults.

The Crab

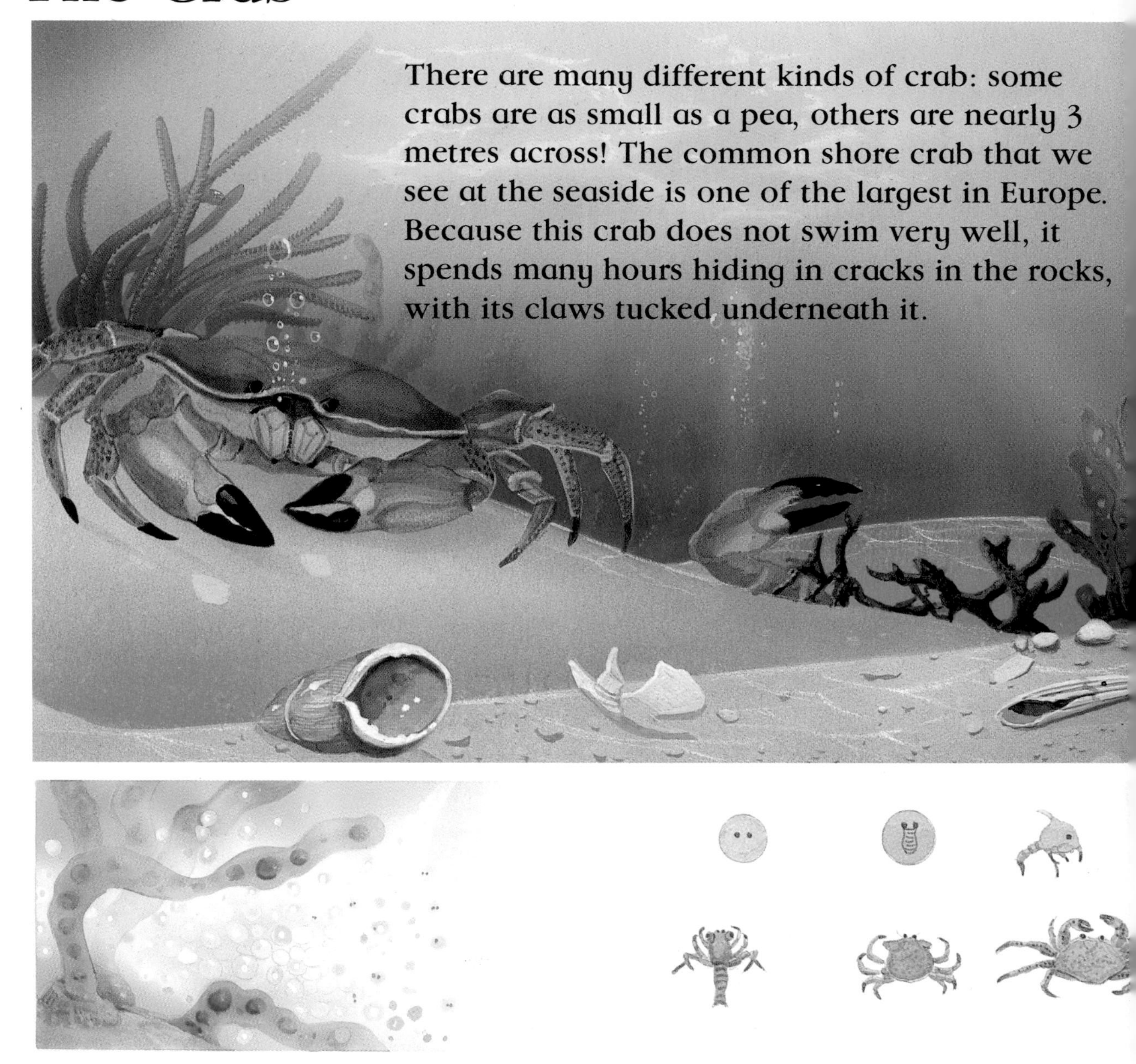

There are many different kinds of crab: some crabs are as small as a pea, others are nearly 3 metres across! The common shore crab that we see at the seaside is one of the largest in Europe. Because this crab does not swim very well, it spends many hours hiding in cracks in the rocks, with its claws tucked underneath it.

The female crab lays many thousands of eggs. These are laid directly into the water or are carried around in a special pouch.

The eggs become *larvae*, and those that survive go through *metamorphosis* many times before becoming adult crabs.

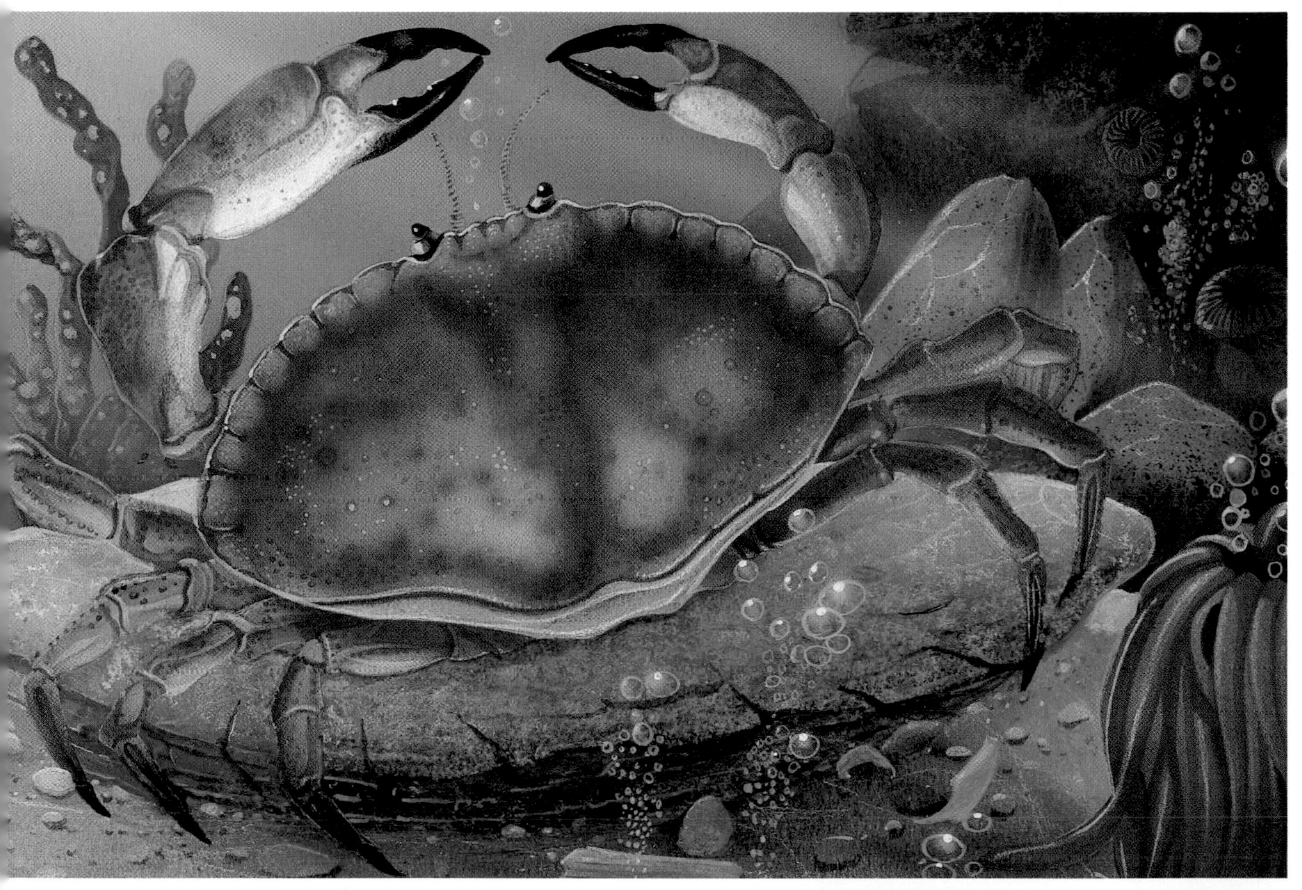

A crab must *moult* several times in order to grow. It sheds its old shell so that its body can develop. This is the most dangerous time for a crab because its body is soft and unprotected. It needs to hide away until the new shell has formed.

The Butterfly

The caterpillar eats leaves from the minute it is born and grows very quickly. Soon its skin becomes too tight. The caterpillar then sheds its skin and eats it, and grows a new skin.

When resting, many caterpillars take on the shape of a twig or a leaf so that *predators* cannot see them.

A butterfly begins life as an egg. A caterpillar hatches from the egg. Each caterpillar has 12 tiny eyes, 8 pairs of legs and 2 short feelers.

fter some weeks, the caterpillar attaches self upside down to a twig or leaf. Next, it ›ins a sort of silky case around itself. This called a chrysalis. The caterpillar turns ıto a butterfly inside the chrysalis.

When the butterfly is ready to emerge, the chrysalis breaks open and the adult butterfly pushes its way out. As soon as its wings are completely dry, it flies away.

The Frog

The tadpole uses its *gills* to breathe under water, like a fish.

Little by little, the tadpole's hind and front legs develop.

The female frog lays a great many eggs which eventually turn into tadpoles. These *larvae*, which feed on water plants, have a large head and a long tail.

At last, the long tail disappears and the tadpole develops lungs. It begins to breathe air.

After this transformation, which takes about 4 months, the tadpole has turned into a frog.

The Horse

At birth, a foal weighs between 40 and 60 kilograms. As soon as it is born, the foal staggers to its feet and begins to suckle from its mother.

A foal can drink between 8 and 20 litres of milk a day. After 3 months it begins to eat grass. By 6 months it is *weaned*.

The mare has only one foal at a time and carries it for about 11 months before giving birth. The foal is usually born in early spring. It is surrounded by a pouch of fluid which it must tear open in order to breathe. The mare then licks the foal to dry it and to stimulate its breathing.

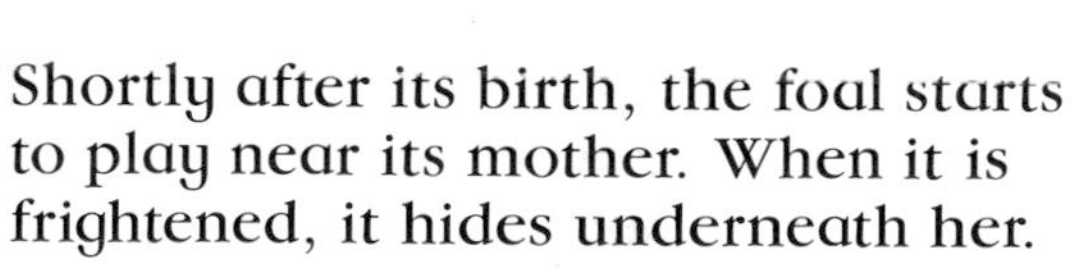

Shortly after its birth, the foal starts to play near its mother. When it is frightened, it hides underneath her.

The foal continues to grow until it is 4 years old. It builds up its muscles by galloping and by jumping up and down.

The Whale

The whale is a marine *mammal*. The female gives birth every 2 or 3 years, and never to more than one calf at a time. Some whales move to warm waters to give birth. The baby whale, called a calf, is born tail-first.

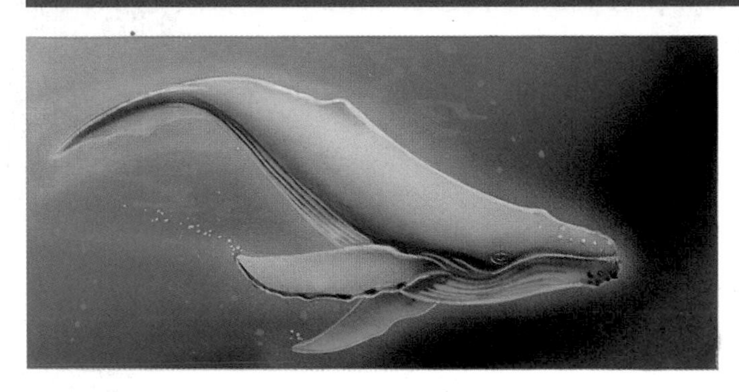

At birth, the calf is already a giant. Some species of whale can be 7 metres long and weigh more than 1000 kilograms when born.

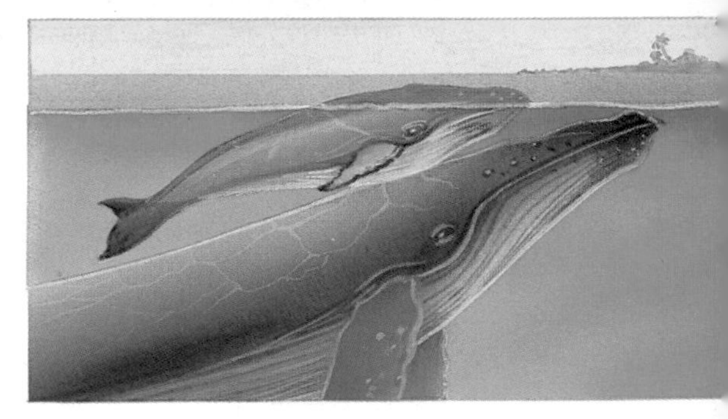

As soon as the calf is born, the mother whale manoeuvres it on to her back an lifts it to the surface so that it can take its first breath.

When the calf is hungry, it rubs against its mother's teats to release a stream of rich, nourishing milk. A baby whale drinks 500 litres of milk a day and grows so quickly that some babies gain over 90 kilograms a day! The calf is *weaned* by the time it is 7 months old, but it will remain with its mother for the next year or two.

The Turtle

Most turtles go ashore to lay their eggs in a deep hole in the sand. After 7 or 8 weeks, the eggs hatch and the baby turtles make for the sea as fast as they can.

The shell of a newborn turtle is still soft, and even though the baby turtles run very quickly, many of them are caught and eaten by seabirds. The lucky ones reach the sea, where they will grow into adults.

Using her hind legs, it takes the turtle almost 5 hours to dig out th hole where she will lay her round, white eggs.

The baby turtle hatches after several weeks. It forces its way out of the shell by using a tooth at the end of its snout.

Baby turtles have to break through their shells and make their way to the sea without any help at all from the adults.

The Tree

In spring, rain makes the seeds in the ground swell. Next, a root appears and a shoot sprouts through the earth. The plant begins to grow and leaves start to develop. Little by little, the tree gets bigger. Then it flowers.

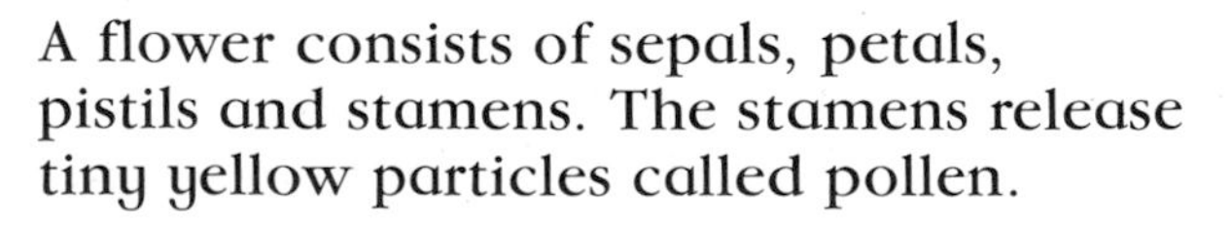

A flower consists of sepals, petals, pistils and stamens. The stamens release tiny yellow particles called pollen.

Pollen is carried away by wind, birds and insects. It lands on the pistil of another flower and pollination, or fertilisation, takes place.

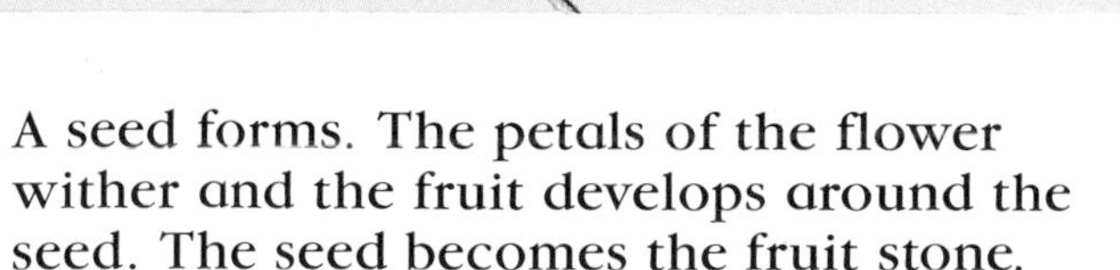

A seed forms. The petals of the flower wither and the fruit develops around the seed. The seed becomes the fruit stone.

The fruit ripens and falls from the tree. If the fruit stone takes root in the earth, a new fruit tree will grow from it.

The Salmon

An adult salmon lives in the sea, but returns to the stream where it was born in order to lay its eggs. To do this, it swims up rivers and jumps over rapids and waterfalls, without stopping to feed. Many salmon die during this long and dangerous journey.

After reaching the place where they were born, the females lay their eggs in gravel on the bed of the stream.

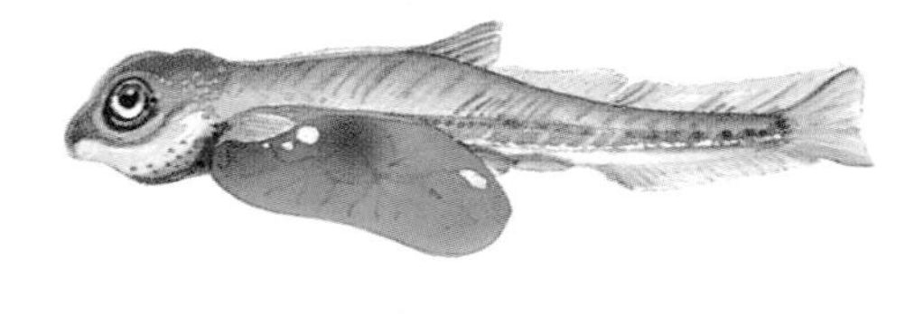

The eggs hatch after about 3 months. A baby salmon is called a parr. Many of them are eaten by fish or birds.

ıose that survive spend the next 2 or 3
ːars in the stream where they were born.
ıen they make their way to the ocean.

Some years later, when they are adults, they will return to the place where they were born to lay their own eggs.

The Koala Bear

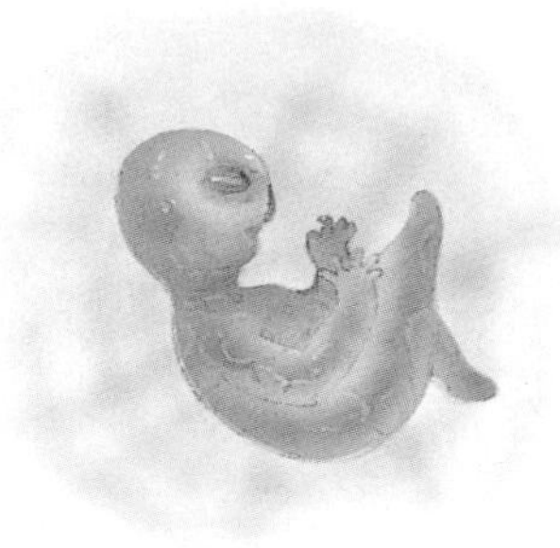

The baby is pink and hairless, its eyes and ears are closed, and its back legs are barely formed.

This tiny blind creature has to find its way to its mother's pouch all by itself. There, where it is sheltered and warm, the baby will grow by feeding on its mother's milk.

Like the kangaroo, the koala bear has a pouch on its stomach where the baby koala spends the first 8 months of its life. When newly born, a baby koala is very tiny – no bigger than a cherry stone!

ter 6 months, the young koala easures 20 centimetres and weighs out 500 grams. It is covered in hair d starts to venture outside the pouch.

At 8 months, it stays outside the pouch for good. By now it is too large to get back inside! When the koala is a year old, it is an adult. Soon afterwards, it leaves its mother.

A Human Being

A human baby develops for 9 months inside a bag of fluid in its mother's womb. During this time, the mother feeds the baby through the *umbilical cord*. Then the baby is born, and for the first few months of life it usually feeds entirely on its mother's milk.

The baby grows larger and learns how to sit, how to walk, and how to eat solid food. It begins to talk, to discover the world around it, to read and to write.

After its sixth birthday, a child's milk teeth are gradually replaced by 28 proper teeth. Later, 4 *wisdom teeth* will appear.

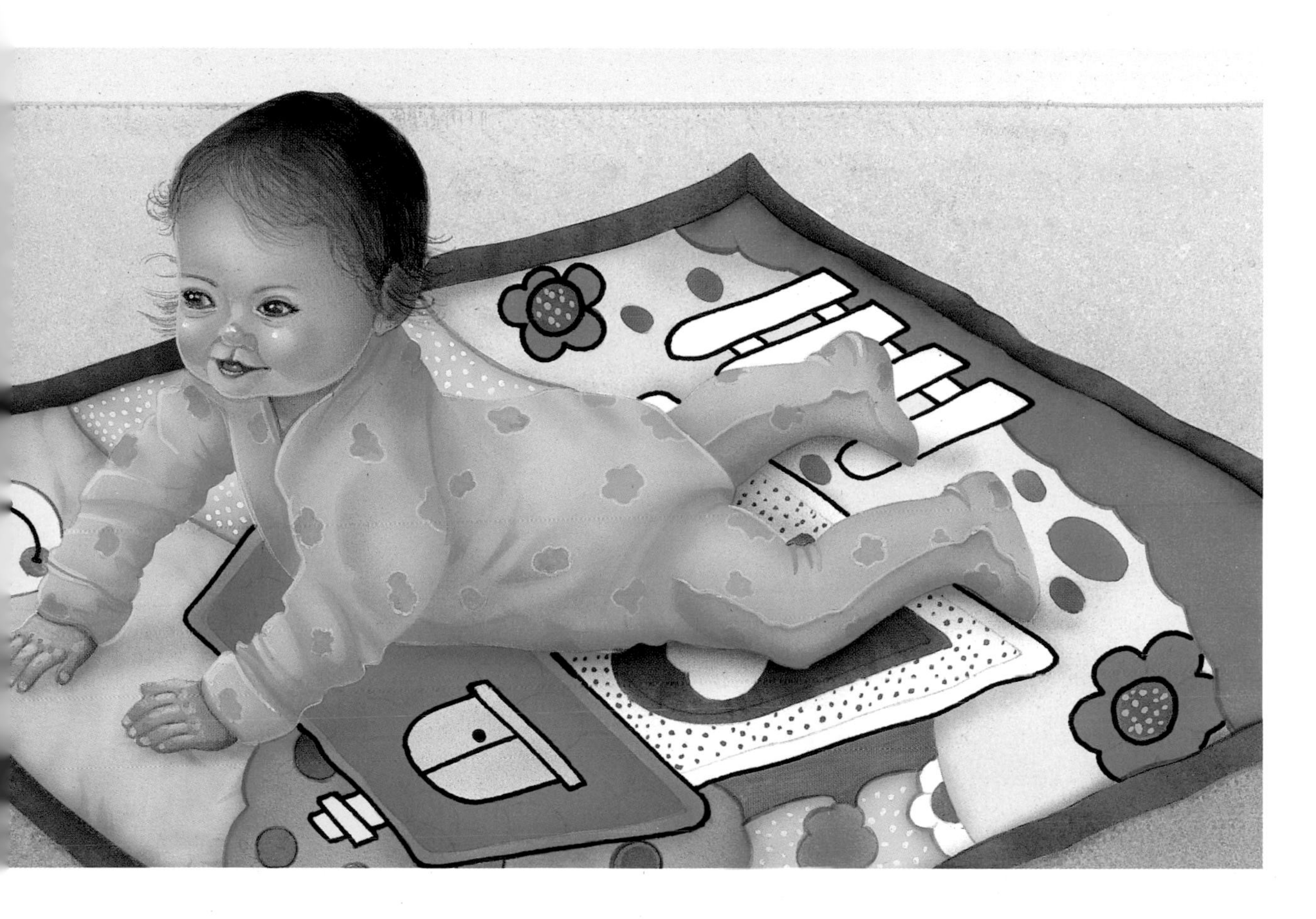

Puberty occurs between the ages of 12 and 16. In girls, the breasts and hips start to take shape. In boys, hair starts to grow on the face and the voice becomes deeper.

The young human being has become an adult. Soon these young men and women will start work and perhaps have families of their own.

Glossary

Gills
The parts of a fish which filter oxygen from the water. Fish and other creatures breathe by using gills.

Impermeable
Something which does not let in water.

Larva
The stage of development of an insect between an egg and a pupa. Larvae look very different from adult insects.

Mammal
An animal that feeds its young with its own milk. The elephant, the dog and the whale are mammals. So are humans.

Metamorphosis
An important transformation. For example, when a caterpillar turns into a butterfly, it has undergone metamorphosis.

To moult
When an animal changes its hair, its feathers, its skin or its shell, we say it is moulting.

Predator
An animal that hunts or kills other animals for food.

Umbilical cord
The cord by which a baby is able to feed whilst in its mother's womb.

To wean
To stop giving milk to a baby or a small animal gradually so that it starts to eat solid food.

Wisdom teeth
The four large teeth which appear after all the other teeth.